ABDO
Publishing Company

RESPIRATORY
System

BODY SYSTEMS

A Buddy Book by **Sarah Tieck**

VISIT US AT
www.abdopublishing.com

Printed in the United States of America, North Mankato, Minnesota.
092010
012011
 PRINTED ON RECYCLED PAPER

Coordinating Series Editor: Rochelle Baltzer
Contributing Editors: Megan M. Gunderson, BreAnn Rumsch, Marcia Zappa
Graphic Design: Jenny Christensen
Cover Photograph: *iStockphoto*: ©iStockphoto.com/mrPliskin.
Interior Photographs/Illustrations: *AP Photo*: Matt Dunham (p. 13); *Eight Street Studio* (p. 22); *Fotosearch*: Fotosearch Stock (p. 19), *iStockphoto*: ©iStockphoto.com/ahmed717 (p. 22), ©iStockphoto.com/emreogan (p. 27), ©iStockphoto.com/kickstand (p. 29), ©iStockphoto.com/lance71 (p. 23), ©iStockphoto.com/LindseyJohnson1 (p. 23), ©iStockphoto.com/monkeybusinessimages (pp. 7, 19), ©iStockphoto.com/nicolesy (p. 5), ©iStockphoto.com/stevecoleccs (p. 27), ©iStockphoto.com/ugurbariskan (p. 9); *Photo Researchers, Inc.*: Biophoto Associates (p. 17), BSIP (p. 17), Carlyn Iverson (p. 11); *Shutterstock*: Heath Doman (p. 30), Gelpi (p. 9), Sebastian Kaulitzki (pp. 15, 21), Levent Konuk (p. 25), Juriah Mosin (p. 7), zhuda (p. 9).

Library of Congress Cataloging-in-Publication Data

Tieck, Sarah, 1976-
  Respiratory system / Sarah Tieck.
    p. cm. -- (Body systems)
  ISBN 978-1-61613-501-0
  1. Respiratory organs--Juvenile literature. 2. Respiration--Juvenile literature. I. Title.
QP121.T52 2011
612.2--dc22

                          2010019652

Table of Contents

Amazing Body 4

Working Together 6

Breathe In 8

Make Some Noise 12

Lungs 14

An Even Trade 18

Brain Food 22

Sniffle Sniffle 24

An Important System 28

Healthy Body Files 30

Important Words 31

Web Sites 31

Index 32

WORD OF MOUTH

Amazing Body

Your body is amazing! It does thousands of things each day. Your body parts help you run, smell, and talk.

Groups of body parts make up body systems. Each system does important work. The respiratory system allows you to breathe. Let's learn more about it!

Your respiratory system is located in your head, neck, and chest.

Working Together

When you breathe, many things happen at once. Your brain tells your body what to do. You don't even have to think about doing it!

As you breathe in, fresh air fills your lungs. A gas called oxygen enters your body. Oxygen gives your body **energy**.

As you breathe out, your lungs let out used air. A gas called carbon dioxide leaves with it.

WORD OF MOUTH

Plants make oxygen and let it out into the air.

Your body works hard to breathe while you are running. This strengthens your lungs.

During normal breathing, people take in about one pint (.5 L) of air with each breath.

Breathe In

Breathing starts with your nose and mouth. Both body parts can let air in and out.

Air that enters your mouth goes straight into your throat. Air that goes through your nose passes through the nasal cavity. This is a large area behind your nose.

Inside the nasal cavity, tiny hairs and **mucus** trap harmful matter. Air becomes warm and wet. Later, this will **protect** the lungs.

8

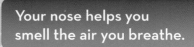

Your nose helps you smell the air you breathe.

From your nasal cavity, the warm, wet air moves through the throat, or pharynx. This long, **muscular** tube is lined with **mucus**. It traps harmful matter, just like the nasal cavity.

The epiglottis is a small flap that covers the larynx. It opens to let air into the larynx. From there, air moves into the trachea. Finally, it enters the lungs.

How It Sounds

pharynx (FA-rihnks)
epiglottis (eh-puh-GLA-tuhs)
larynx (LEHR-ihnks)
trachea (TRAY-kee-uh)

YOUR RESPIRATORY SYSTEM

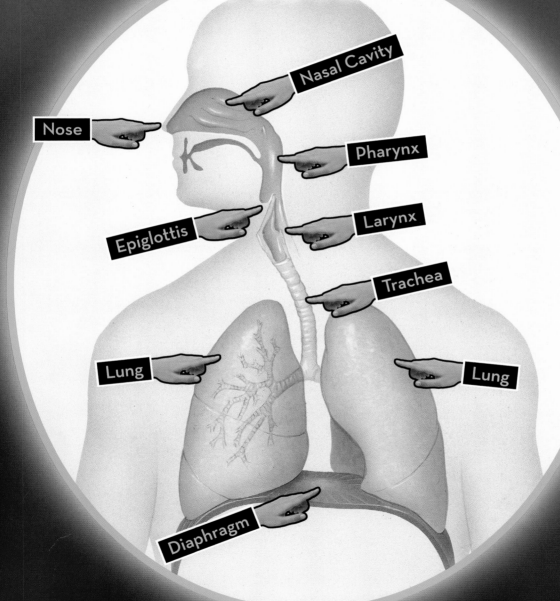

Nasal Cavity

Nose

Pharynx

Epiglottis

Larynx

Trachea

Lung

Lung

Diaphragm

Make Some Noise

Your vocal cords are below your epiglottis. They let you speak and sing.

First, tiny **muscles** stretch the vocal cords and move them close together. Then, air from the lungs is pushed through them. The cords **vibrate**, which makes sounds. Your tongue, lips, and teeth turn the sounds into words.

Opera singers train their vocal cord and diaphragm muscles to help them control their sound.

WORD OF MOUTH

Lungs

The trachea sends air to your right lung and your left lung. Lungs are spongy and light. They are **protected** by your ribs.

The diaphragm is a large **muscle** below the lungs. When it tightens, you breathe in. When it relaxes, you breathe out.

How It Sounds

diaphragm (DEYE-uh-fram)

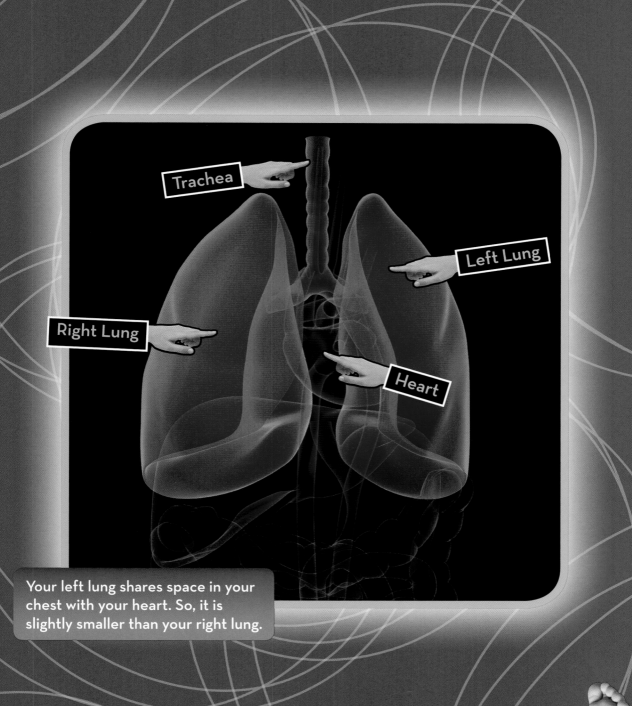

Trachea

Left Lung

Right Lung

Heart

Your left lung shares space in your chest with your heart. So, it is slightly smaller than your right lung.

Lungs have hundreds of millions of alveoli!

WORD OF MOUTH

Air continues moving inside the lungs. The trachea splits into two tubes called bronchi. Each tube leads to one lung. Bronchi lead to smaller and smaller tubes called bronchioles.

On each bronchiole, there are many air sacs called alveoli. They help the lungs get oxygen to your body.

How It Sounds

bronchi (BRAHN-keye)
bronchioles (BRAHN-kee-ohls)
alveoli (al-VEE-uh-leye)

Alveoli are part of
each bronchiole.

Bronchus

Bronchiole

Alveoli

Alveoli are tiny. Their walls
are thinner than tissue paper!

An Even Trade

Alveoli pass oxygen into the blood. They also take carbon dioxide out of the blood. This is the final step in the **process** of respiration. It gives your body **energy**.

In the lungs, blood picks up oxygen. It sends oxygen all over your body to be used for energy.

Alveoli are surrounded by small **blood vessels** called capillaries. Alveoli walls are very thin. When air fills the alveoli, oxygen passes through the walls. It enters the capillaries. Then, blood carries the oxygen all over your body.

At the same time, carbon dioxide leaves the blood. It enters the alveoli. From there, carbon dioxide leaves your body. It leaves the body through the same tubes oxygen entered the body.

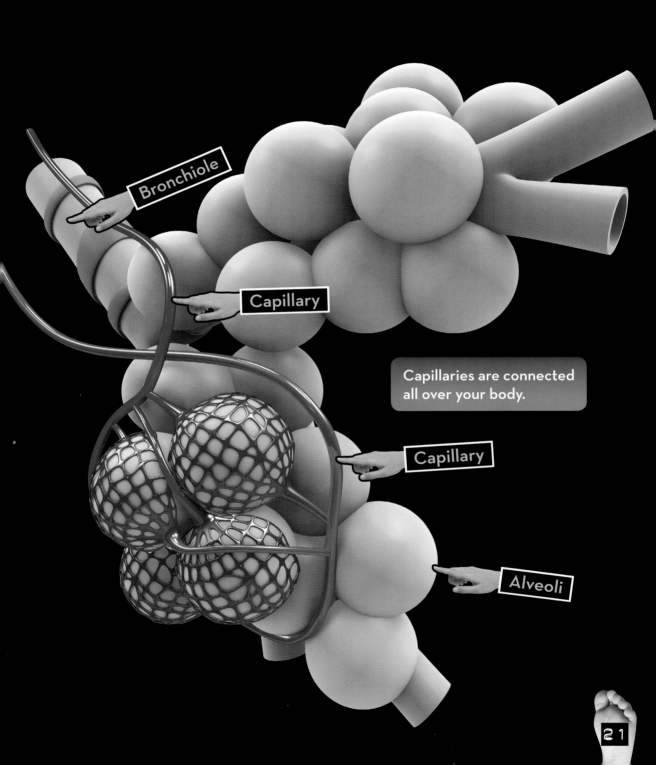

Bronchiole

Capillary

Capillary

Alveoli

Capillaries are connected all over your body.

21

Brain Food

Does your mom or dad snore?

Even while you sleep, your body keeps breathing. Snoring happens when the mouth and throat **muscles** relax. As air passes through, the relaxed parts **vibrate**. That makes the snoring sound!

Feeling sleepy?

A yawn is when you open your mouth wide and breathe deeply. No one knows for sure why people yawn. Many think it brings oxygen into your body when you are bored or tired.

What are hiccups?

Hiccups happen when your diaphragm moves in a jerky way. This forces air toward the lungs. The epiglottis shuts, blocking the air. The air hits the epiglottis and moves the vocal cords. Then you hiccup!

23

If you breathe in dirty or dry air, you might sneeze. When you sneeze, the air travels faster than cars on a highway!

Sniffle Sniffle

Dust, smoke, and **germs** can make your respiratory system sick. Your throat might get sore. Your nose might be full of **mucus**. And, you might have trouble speaking or breathing.

Asthma is a respiratory illness. Breathing in dirty air can cause an asthma attack, making it hard to breathe. Inhalers can help open the airways.

Sometimes you can help your respiratory system heal. Get plenty of rest and drink warm liquids. Crying, coughing, sneezing, or swallowing also help clean your system.

Other times, you may need to visit a doctor. Doctors have tools to hear your lungs. They can also look inside your trachea and bronchioles.

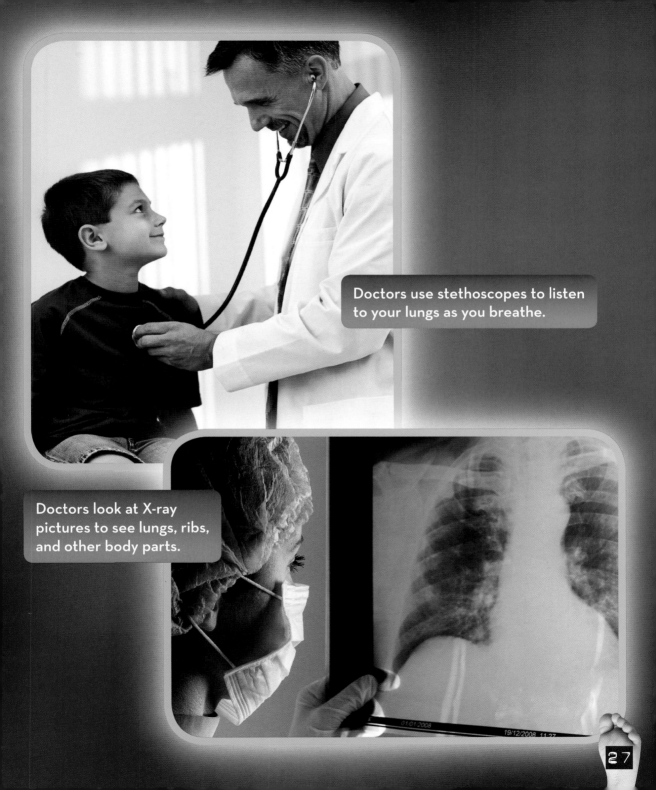

Doctors use stethoscopes to listen to your lungs as you breathe.

Doctors look at X-ray pictures to see lungs, ribs, and other body parts.

An Important System

Think about how much happens when you take just one breath! By learning about your respiratory system, you can **protect** it. Then, you can make good choices to keep your body healthy.

People need oxygen to live.
They can only hold their breath
underwater for a short time.

HEALTHY BODY FILES

STAY WELL

✔ A sneeze can send **germs** several feet from the body. So, sneeze into your arm to keep illnesses from spreading.

✔ Feeling sick? Doctors suggest drinking eight glasses of water each day to be healthy.

DON'T SMOKE

✔ Smoking harms lungs. Keep your lungs strong by avoiding this unhealthy habit.

✔ Breathing in other people's smoke can also be harmful. This is called secondhand smoke.

GET STRONG

✔ Exercise is good for your respiratory system. When you move, your **muscles** need more oxygen and you breathe harder. This strengthens your respiratory system.

✔ Be active! An hour of exercise every day is ideal.

Important Words

blood vessel a tube that carries blood throughout the body.

energy the power or ability to do things.

germs (JUHRMS) harmful organisms that can make people sick.

mucus (MYOO-kuhs) thick, slippery, protective fluid from the body.

muscles (MUH-suhls) body tissues, or layers of cells that help move the body. Something with strong, well-developed muscles is muscular.

process a natural order of actions.

protect (pruh-TEHKT) to guard against harm or danger.

vibrate (VEYE-brayt) to move back and forth very fast.

Web Sites

To learn more about the respiratory system, visit ABDO Publishing Company online. Web sites about the respiratory system are featured on our Book Links page. These links are routinely monitored and updated to provide the most current information available.

www.abdopublishing.com

Index

alveoli **16, 17, 18, 20, 21**

blood **18, 19, 20**

bronchi **16, 17**

bronchioles **16, 17, 21, 26**

capillaries **20, 21**

carbon dioxide **6, 18, 20**

diaphragm **11, 13, 14, 23**

energy **6, 18, 19**

epiglottis **10, 11, 12, 23**

health **7, 24, 25, 26, 27, 28, 30**

larynx **10, 11**

lungs **6, 7, 8, 10, 11, 12, 14, 15, 16, 19, 23, 26, 27, 30**

mouth **8, 22, 23**

mucus **8, 10, 24**

nasal cavity **8, 10, 11**

nose **8, 9, 11, 24**

oxygen **6, 16, 18, 19, 20, 23, 29, 30**

pharynx **8, 10, 11, 22, 24**

respiration **18**

throat. *See pharynx*

trachea **10, 11, 14, 15, 16, 26**

vocal cords **12, 13, 23**